# IN THIS BOOK, YOU CAN BUILD...

## CONSTRUCTION TIPS!

- CAREFULLY REMOVE EACH PAGE BEFORE YOU BEGIN CUTTING.
- FOR A SHARPER FOLD, USE A RULER TO FOLD THE LINE AGAINST.
- FEEL FREE TO USE A GLUE STICK OR TAPE!

CASTLE

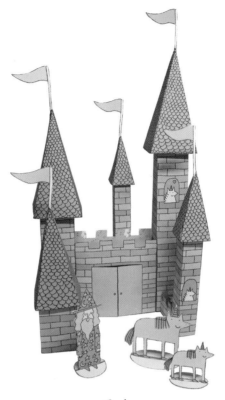

TICKET BOOTH

VENDING MACHINES

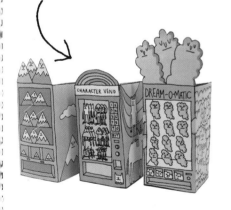

CAROUSEL

ROLLER COASTER

GUESTS

FOOD STAND

+ MORE!

## INSTRUCTIONS!

### STEP 1

GENTLY REMOVE THE PAGE FROM THE BOOK, USING THE PERFORATED LINES.

### STEP 2

SNIP
SNIP
SNIP

CUT OUT EACH OBJECT CAREFULLY. DISCARD THE WHITE AREA OF THE PAGE. EACH OBJECT HAS DIRECTIONS EXPLAINING HOW TO BUILD IT AND PHOTOS SHOWING THE OBJECTS WHEN COMPLETED.

### STEP 3

THE STAR SYMBOL ON EACH FLAP SHOWS WHERE THE GLUE NEEDS TO GO! WHITE STARS ☆ INDICATE TO GLUE ON THE REVERSE SIDE. USE TAPE IF YOU NEED TO STRENGTHEN THE OBJECTS.

### STEP 4

YOU CAN LOOK AT THE DIAGRAMS ON THE FOLLOWING PAGES FOR EXTRA INSTRUCTIONS, BUT MAINLY ... HAVE FUN!

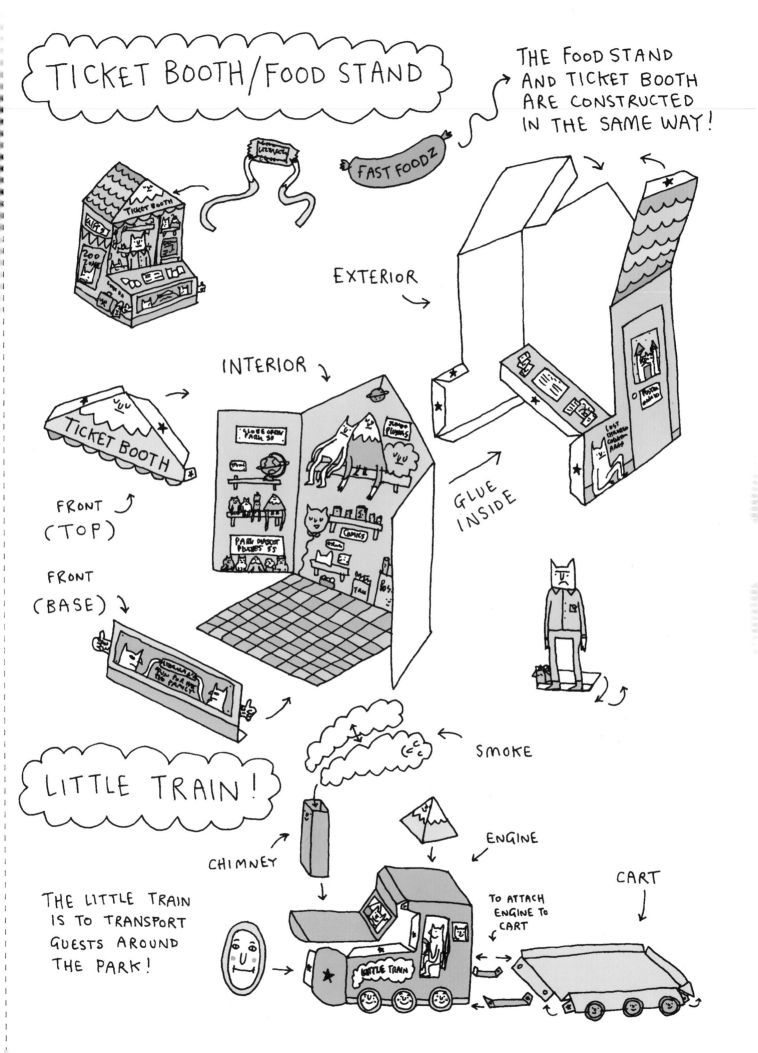

# TICKET BOOTH/FOOD STAND

THE FOOD STAND AND TICKET BOOTH ARE CONSTRUCTED IN THE SAME WAY!

FAST FOODZ

EXTERIOR

INTERIOR

GLUE INSIDE

TICKET BOOTH

FRONT (TOP)

FRONT (BASE)

SMOKE

# LITTLE TRAIN!

THE LITTLE TRAIN IS TO TRANSPORT GUESTS AROUND THE PARK!

CHIMNEY

ENGINE

TO ATTACH ENGINE TO CART

CART

LITTLE TRAIN

 **GUESTS**

 ← THE CAT GUESTS ARE SINGLE SIDED—NO NEED TO GLUE THESE! JUST FOLD THE BASE BACKWARDS TO STAND THEM UP! SOME CATS DON'T HAVE A BASE SO THEY CAN FIT IN THE RIDES.

**CHARACTERS**

FRONT    BACK

FOLD OUT THE FLAPS

GLUE THE PIECES TOGETHER (NOT THE FLAPS!)

NOW YOUR FIGURE WILL STAND! →

THE CHARACTERS ARE DOUBLE-SIDED. THIS BUILDING METHOD APPLIES TO ALL OF THE CHARACTERS (UNICORNS, WIZARD, FROGS, ETC.)

**MOUNTAINS**

**MACHINES**

① ②

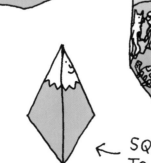

③ ④

THE VENDING MACHINES + THE SPACE CRANE ARE CONSTRUCTED LIKE THIS.

← SQUEEZE MOUNTAINS TO MAKE THEM CONE-SHAPED!

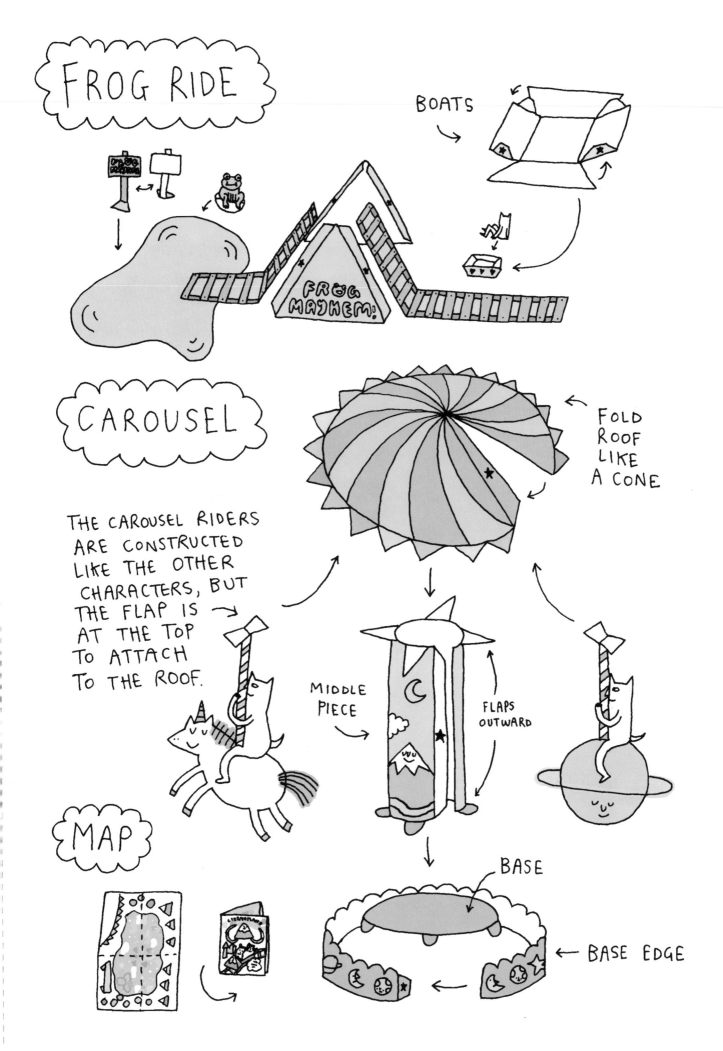

# FROG RIDE

BOATS

FROG MAYHEM!

# CAROUSEL

FOLD ROOF LIKE A CONE

THE CAROUSEL RIDERS ARE CONSTRUCTED LIKE THE OTHER CHARACTERS, BUT THE FLAP IS AT THE TOP TO ATTACH TO THE ROOF.

MIDDLE PIECE

FLAPS OUTWARD

# MAP

BASE

BASE EDGE

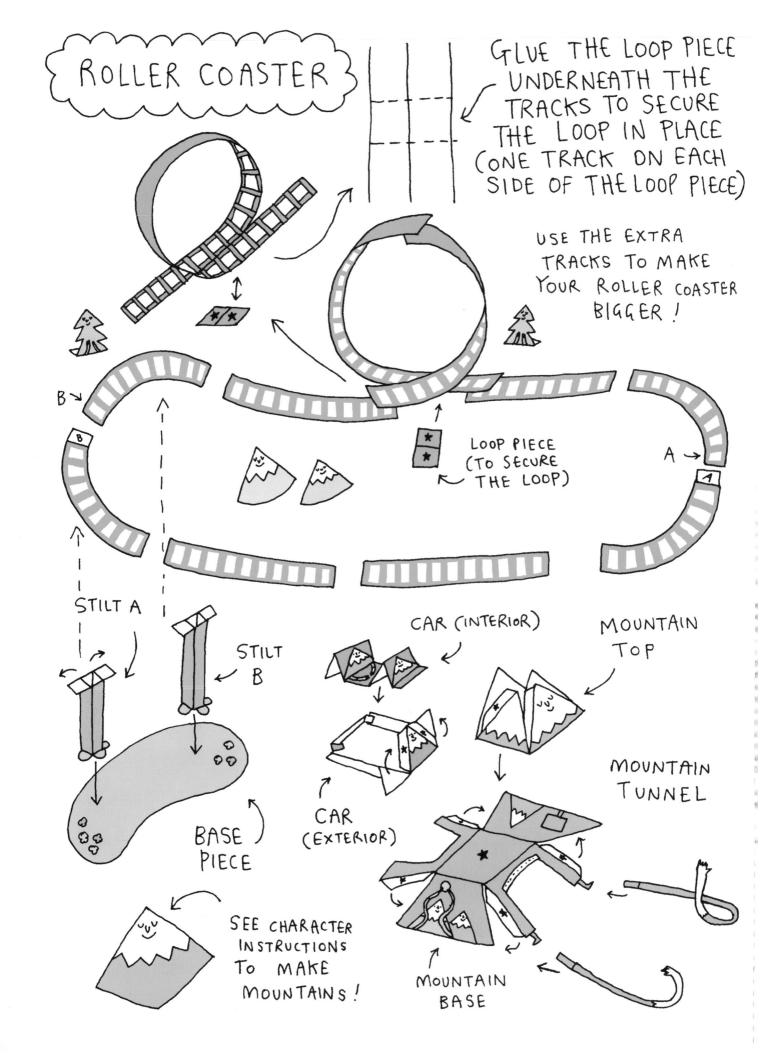

ROLLER COASTER

GLUE THE LOOP PIECE UNDERNEATH THE TRACKS TO SECURE THE LOOP IN PLACE (ONE TRACK ON EACH SIDE OF THE LOOP PIECE)

USE THE EXTRA TRACKS TO MAKE YOUR ROLLER COASTER BIGGER!

LOOP PIECE (TO SECURE THE LOOP)

B

A

STILT A

STILT B

BASE PIECE

CAR (INTERIOR)

CAR (EXTERIOR)

MOUNTAIN TOP

MOUNTAIN TUNNEL

MOUNTAIN BASE

SEE CHARACTER INSTRUCTIONS TO MAKE MOUNTAINS!

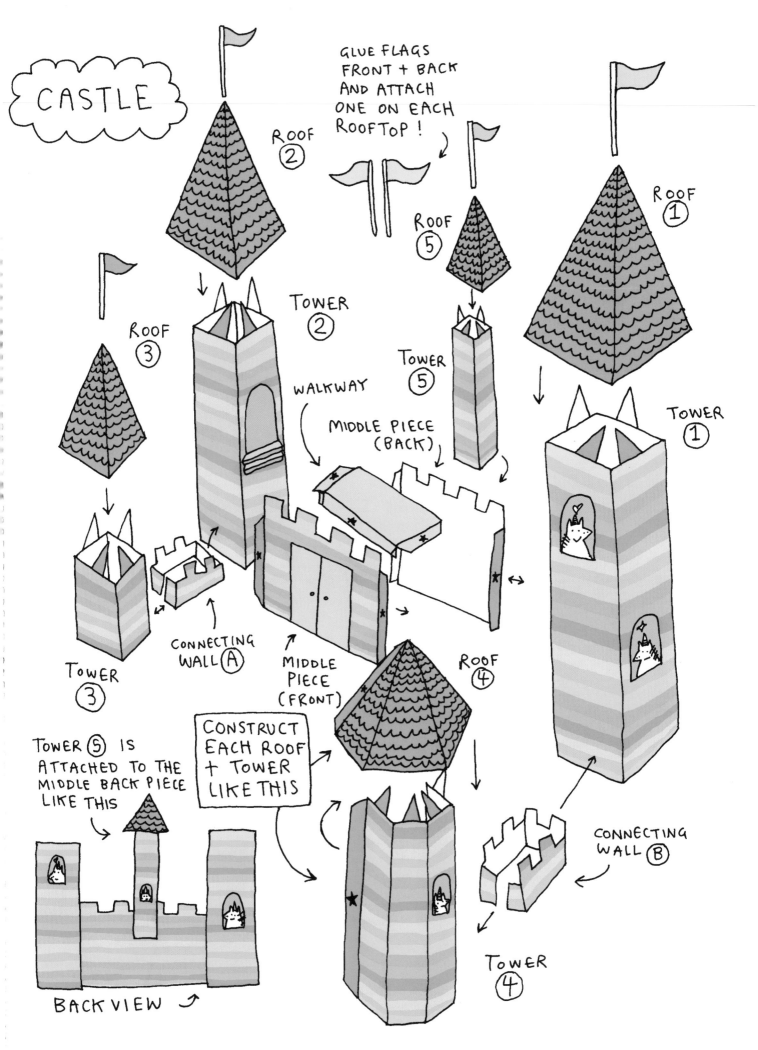

CASTLE

ROOF 2

ROOF 3

ROOF 5

ROOF 1

GLUE FLAGS FRONT + BACK AND ATTACH ONE ON EACH ROOFTOP!

TOWER 2

WALKWAY

MIDDLE PIECE (BACK)

TOWER 5

TOWER 1

CONNECTING WALL A

MIDDLE PIECE (FRONT)

ROOF 4

TOWER 3

TOWER 5 IS ATTACHED TO THE MIDDLE BACK PIECE LIKE THIS

CONSTRUCT EACH ROOF + TOWER LIKE THIS

CONNECTING WALL B

TOWER 4

BACK VIEW →

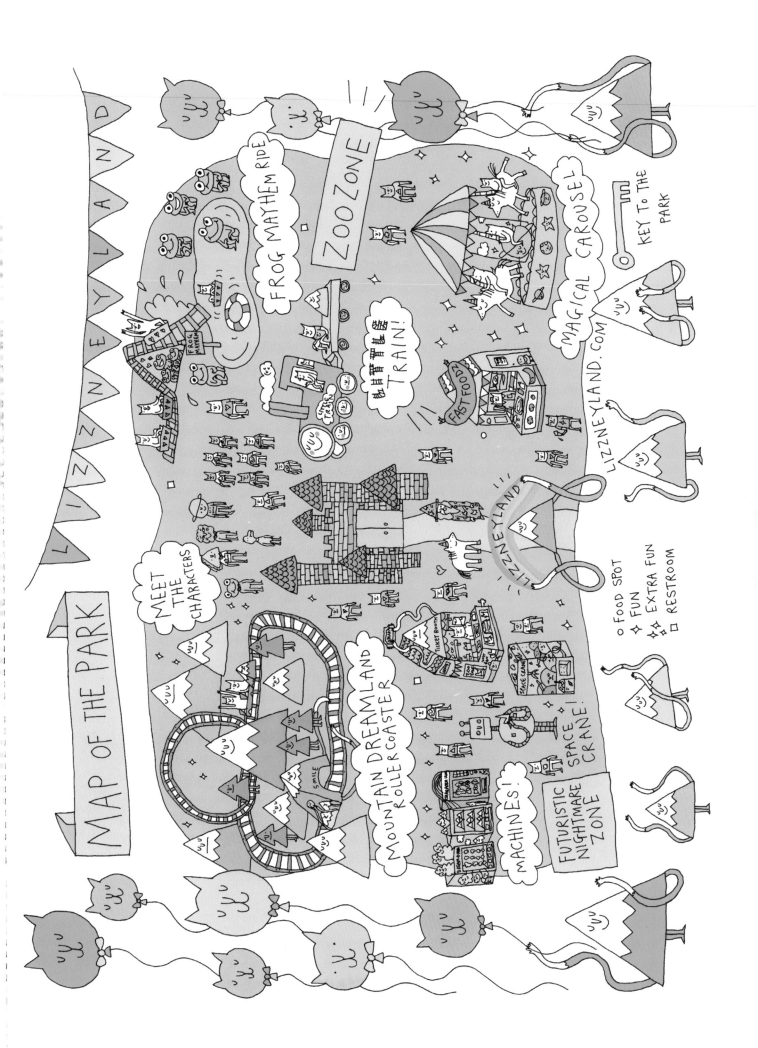

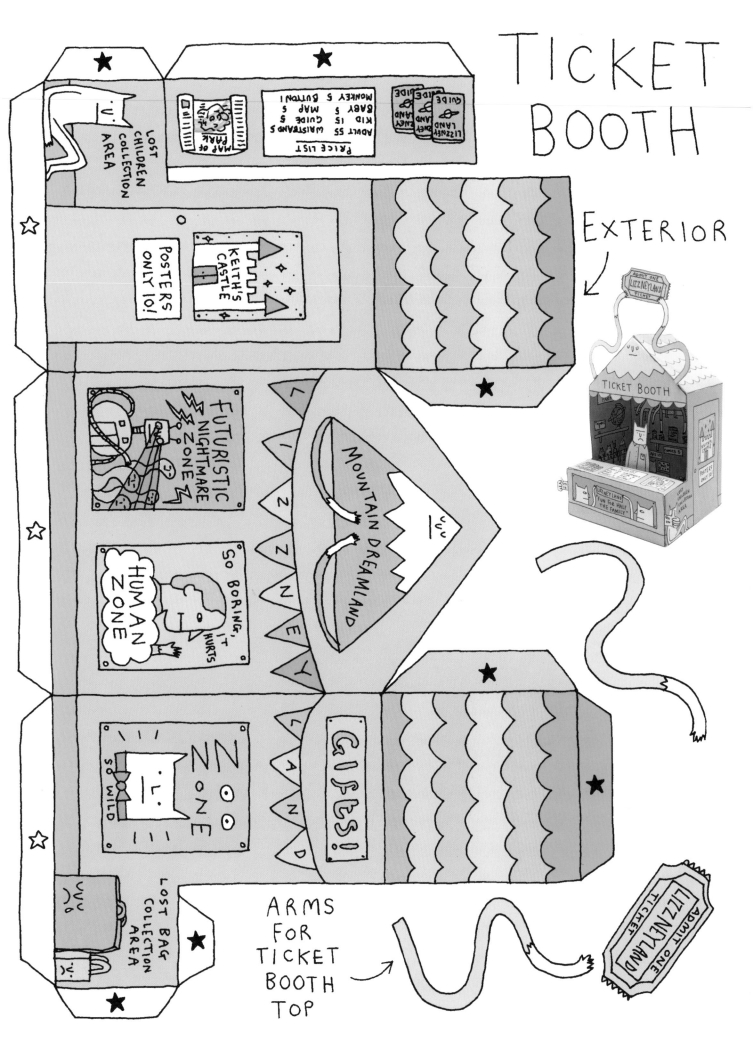

TICKET BOOTH

EXTERIOR

ARMS FOR TICKET BOOTH TOP

# CHARACTERS!

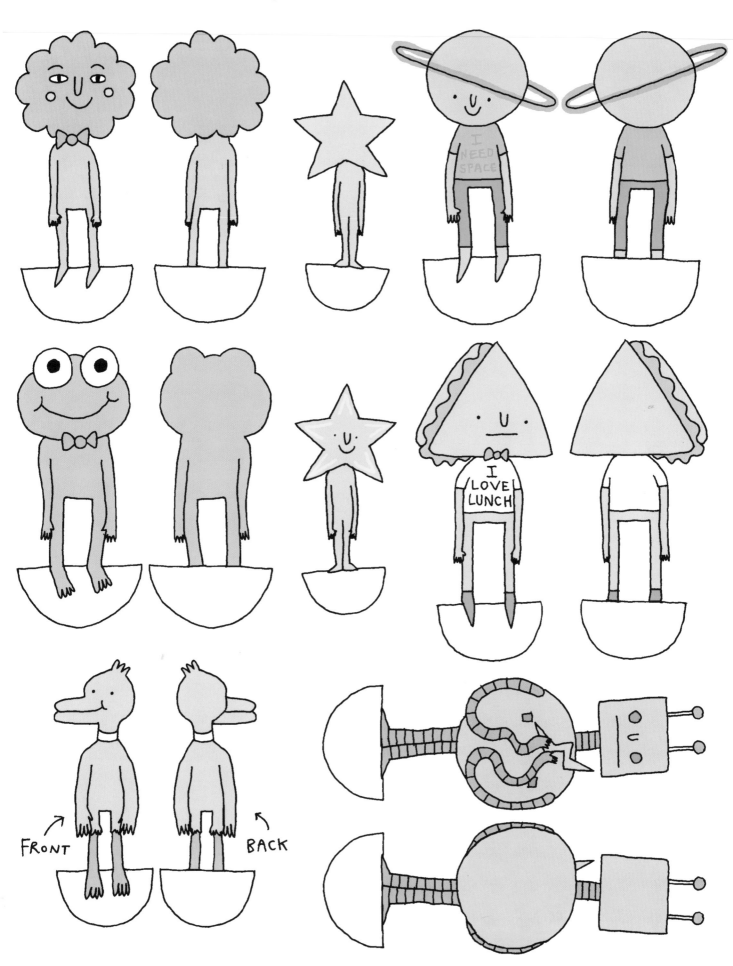

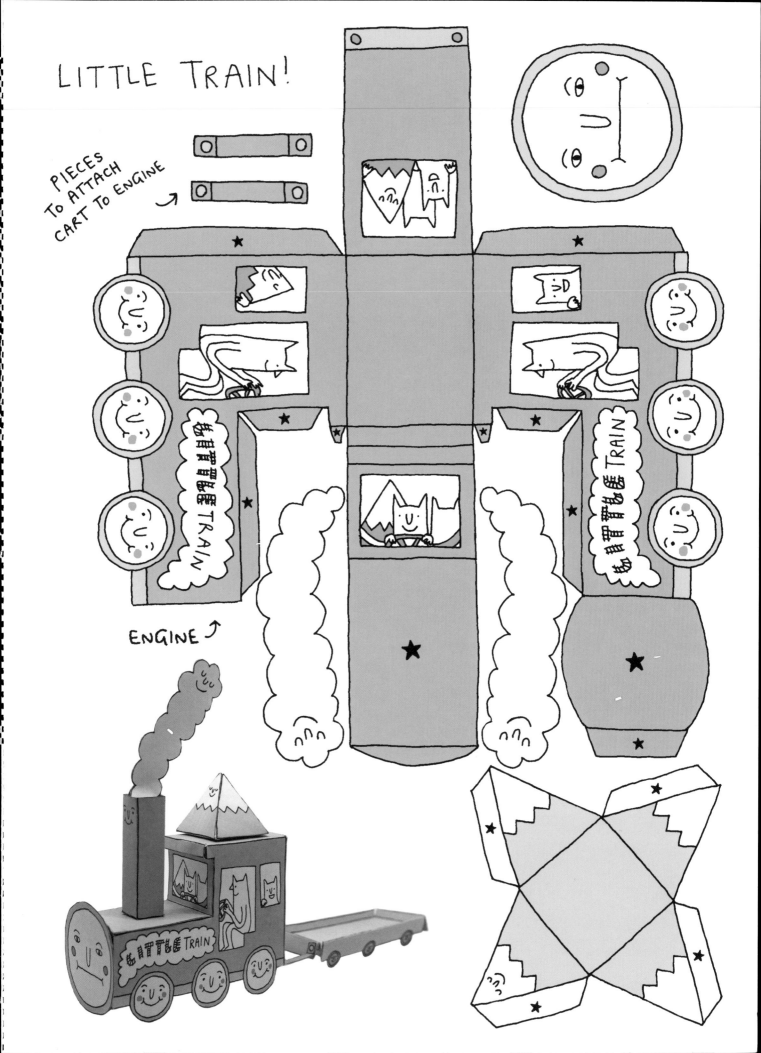

LITTLE TRAIN!

PIECES TO ATTACH CART TO ENGINE

ENGINE

CART

CHIMNEY

LIZZNEYLAND

PARK GUESTS!

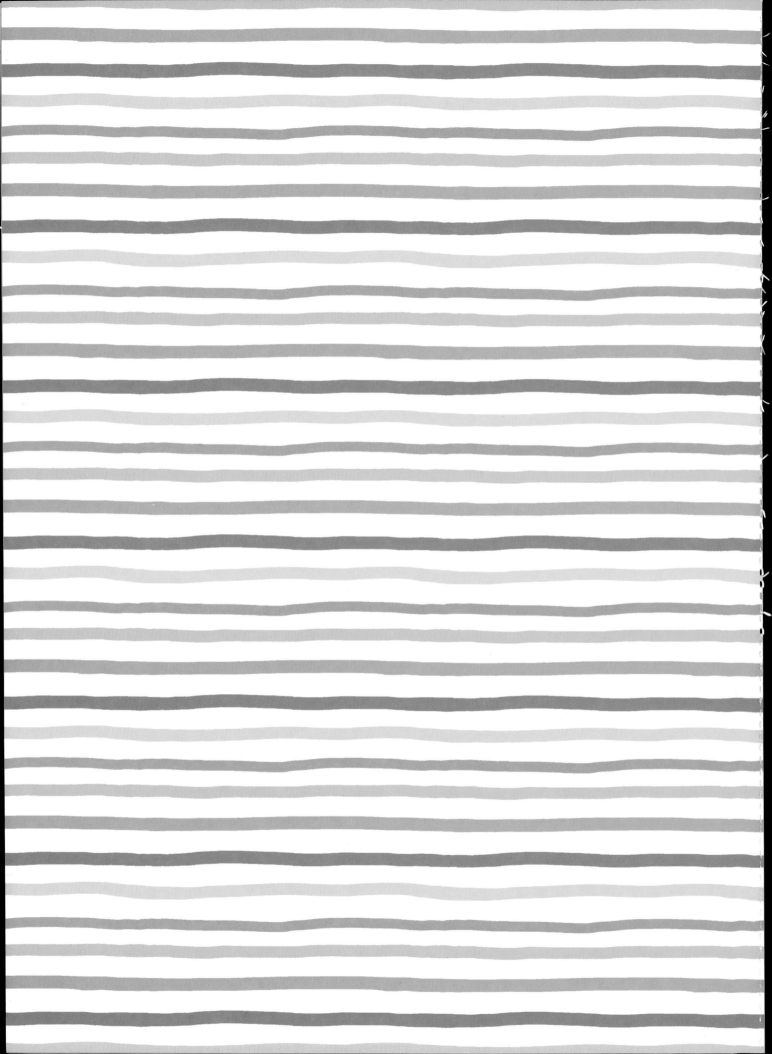

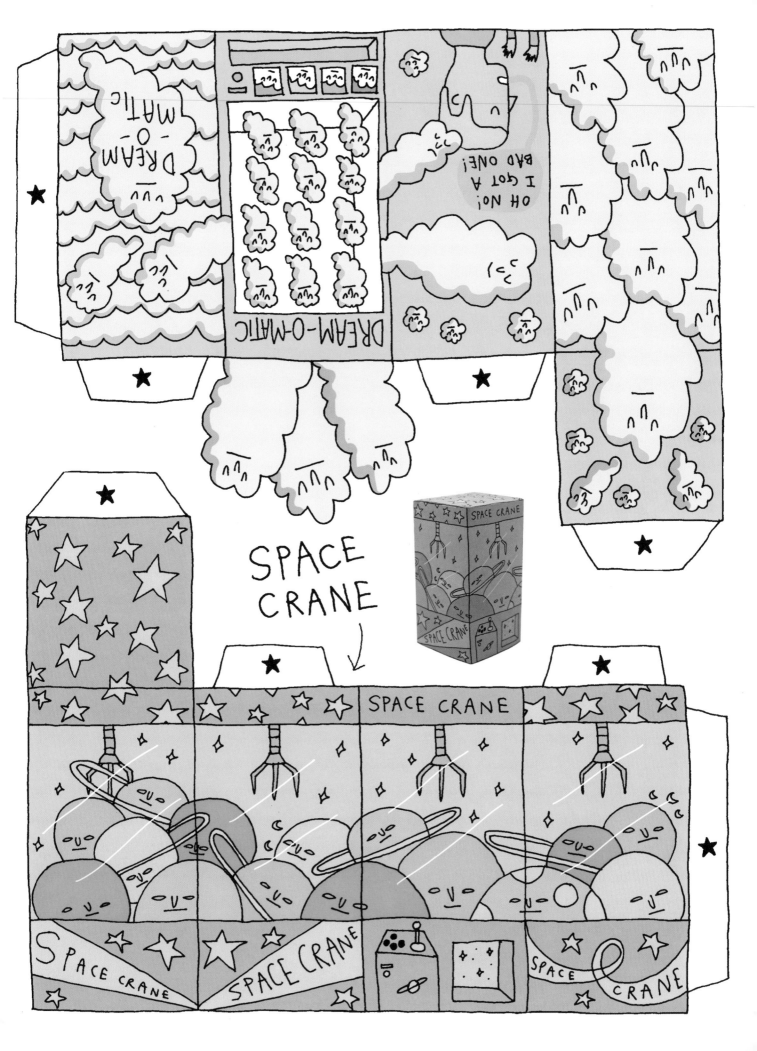

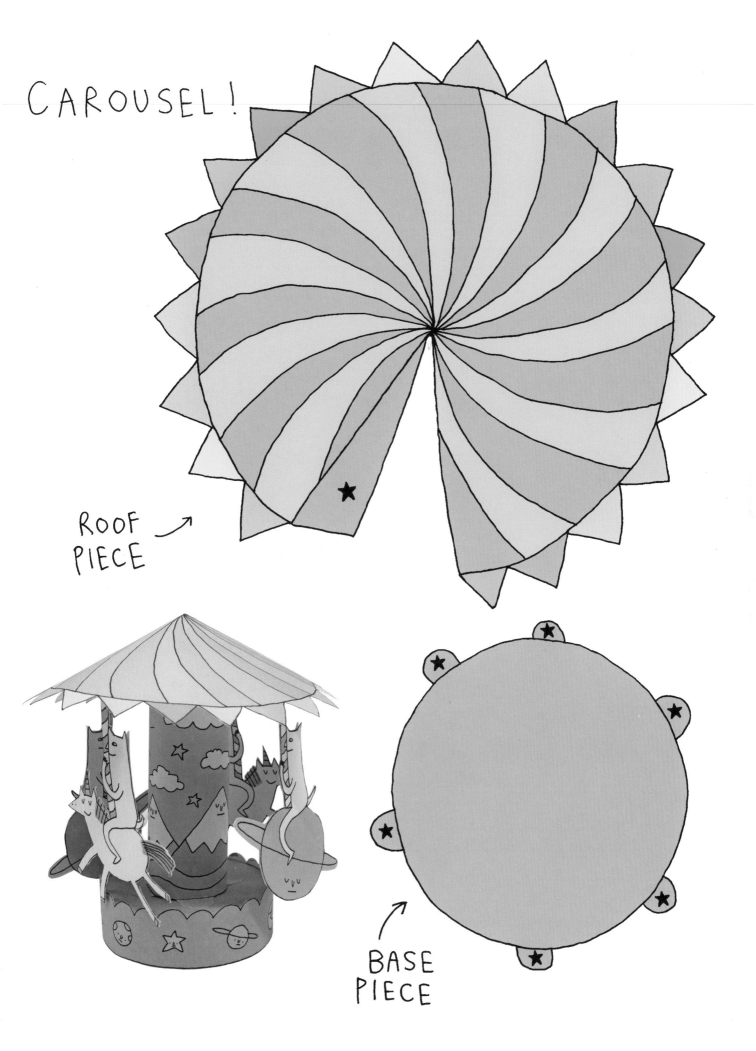

CAROUSEL!

ROOF PIECE →

BASE PIECE

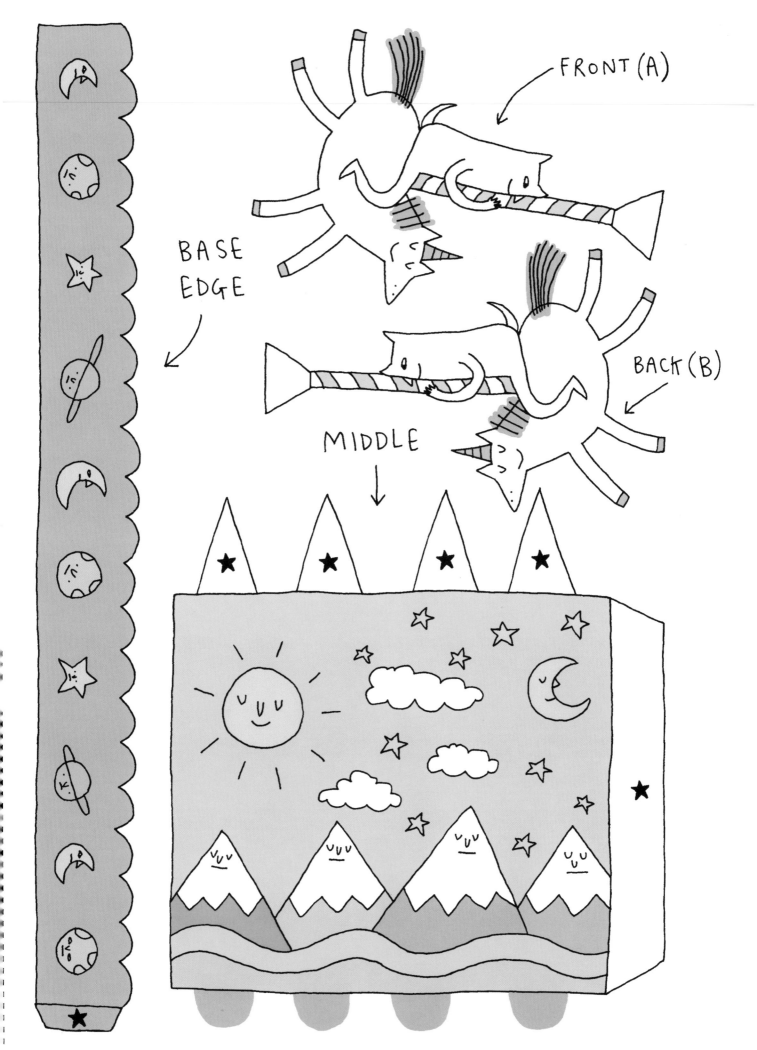

FRONT (A)

BACK (B)

BASE
EDGE

MIDDLE

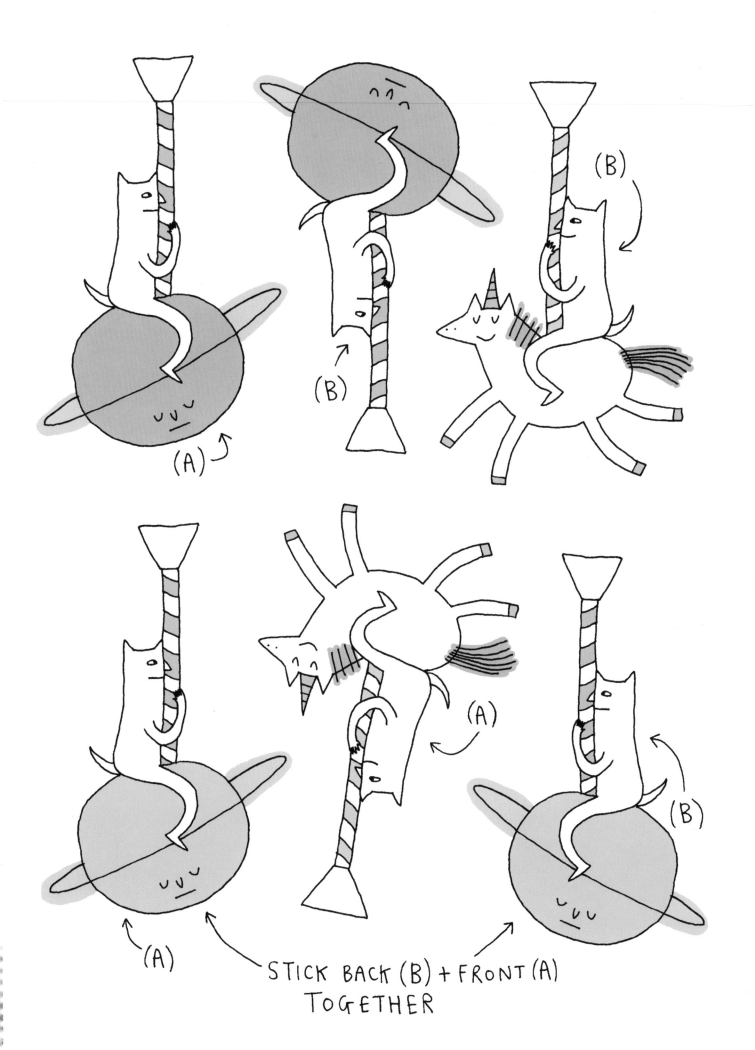

(A)

(B)

(B)

(A)

(A)

(B)

STICK BACK (B) + FRONT (A) TOGETHER

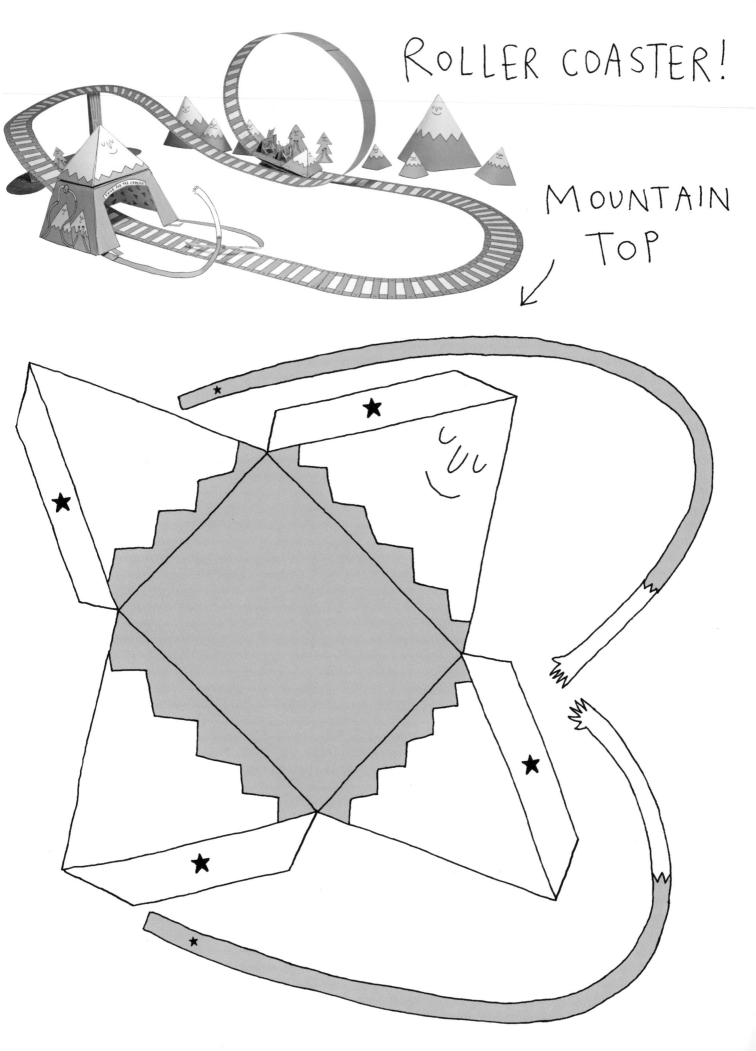

ROLLER COASTER!

MOUNTAIN TOP

MOVING
MOUNTAINS
RIDE

MOUNTAIN
BASE

SMILE FOR THE CAMERA!

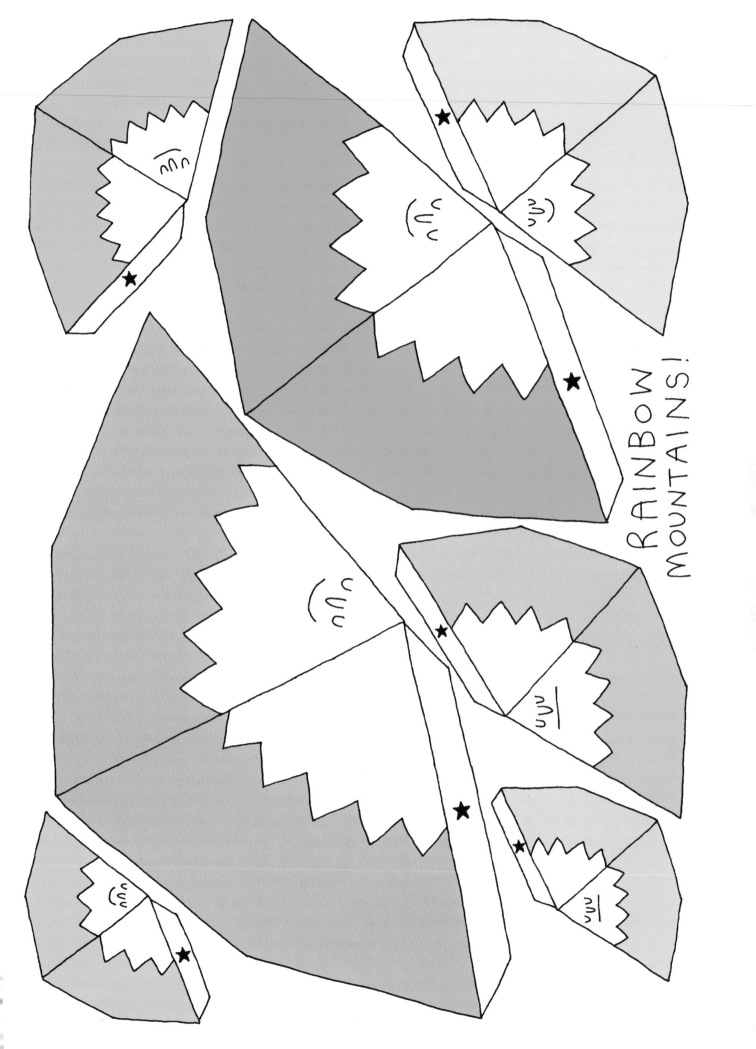

RAINBOW MOUNTAINS!

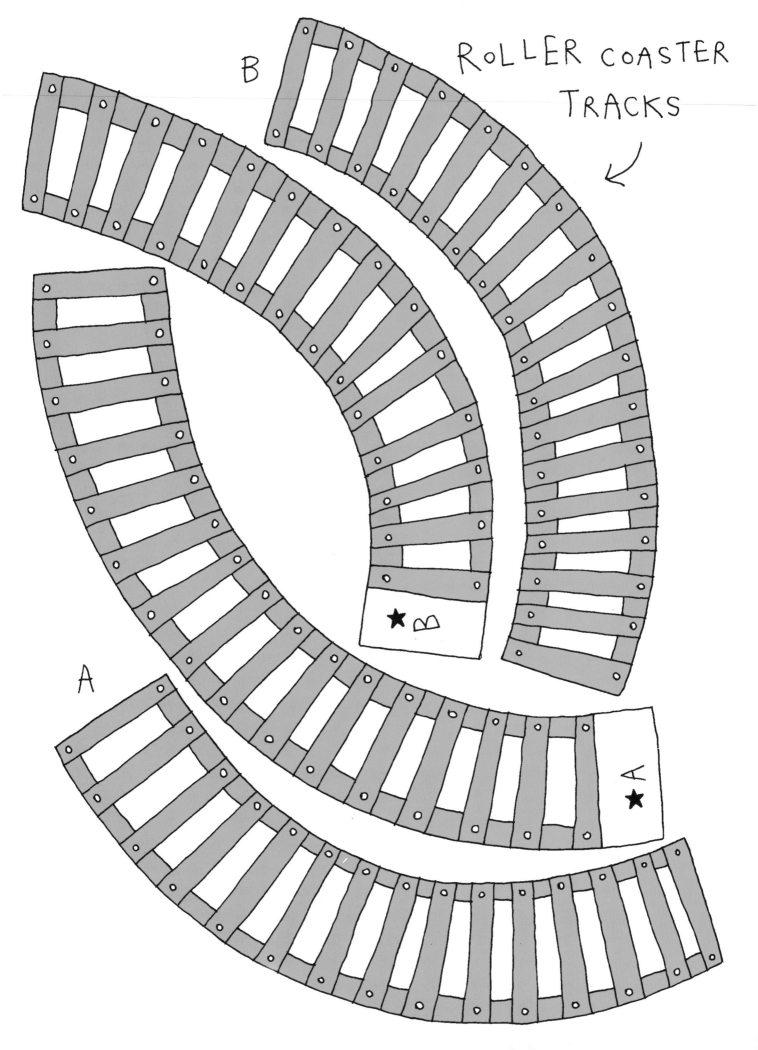

ROLLER COASTER TRACKS

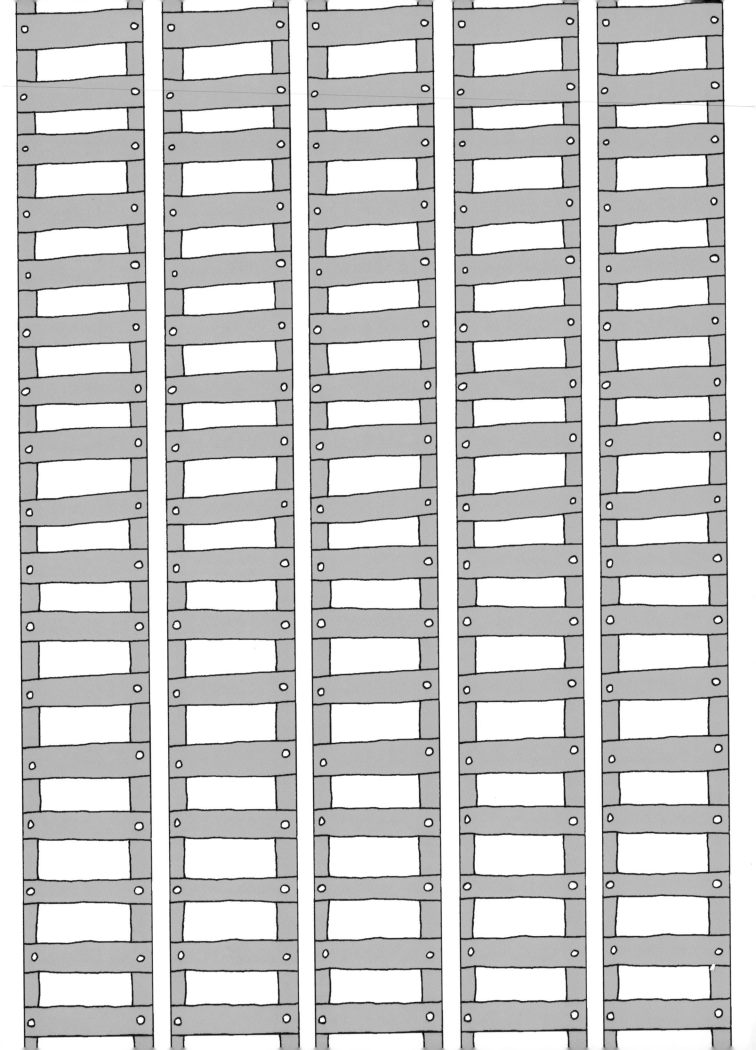

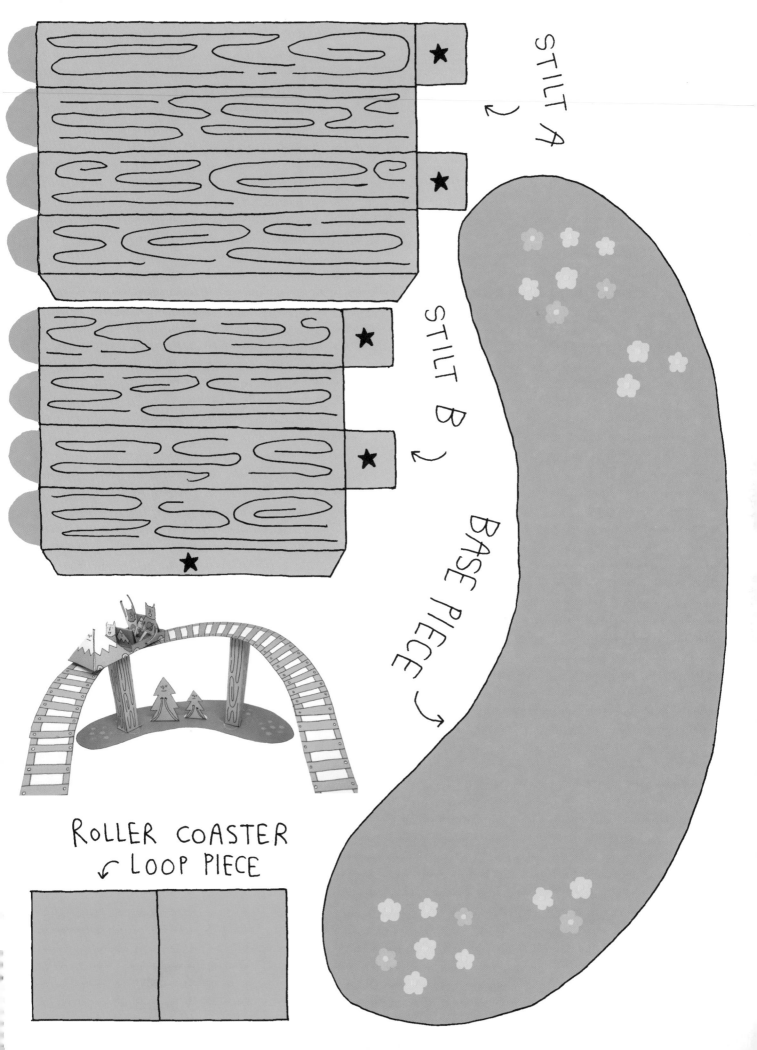

STILT A

STILT B

BASE PIECE

ROLLER COASTER
LOOP PIECE

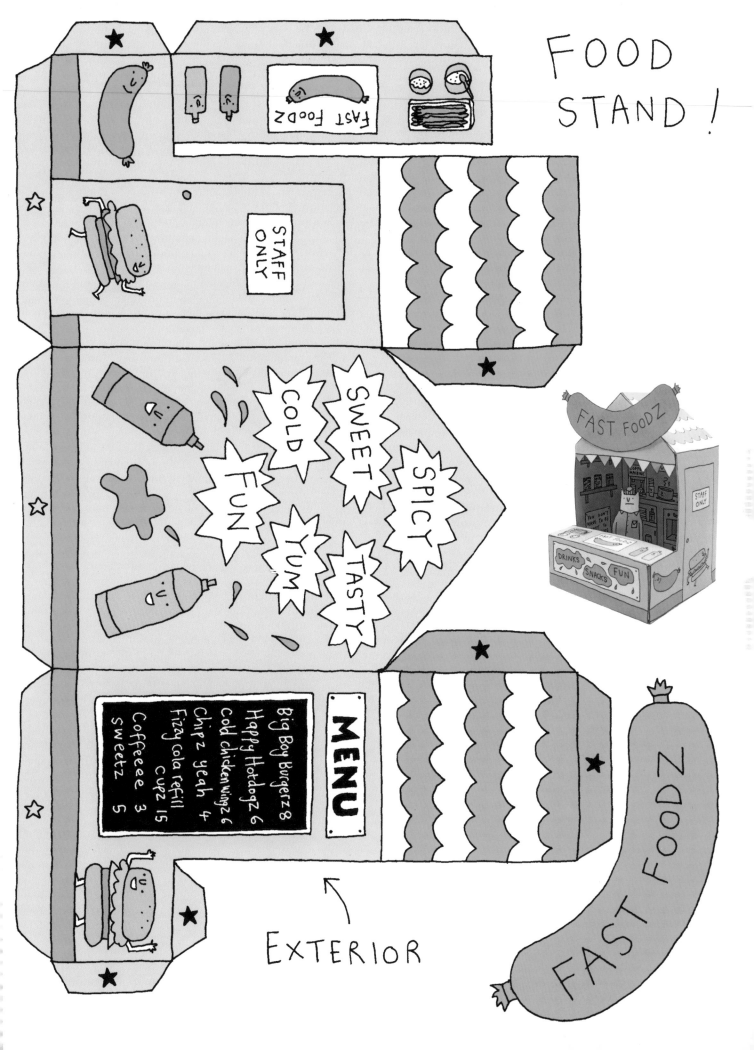

FOOD STAND !

EXTERIOR

# FROG RIDE!

BACK

FRONT

FRÖG MAYHEM!

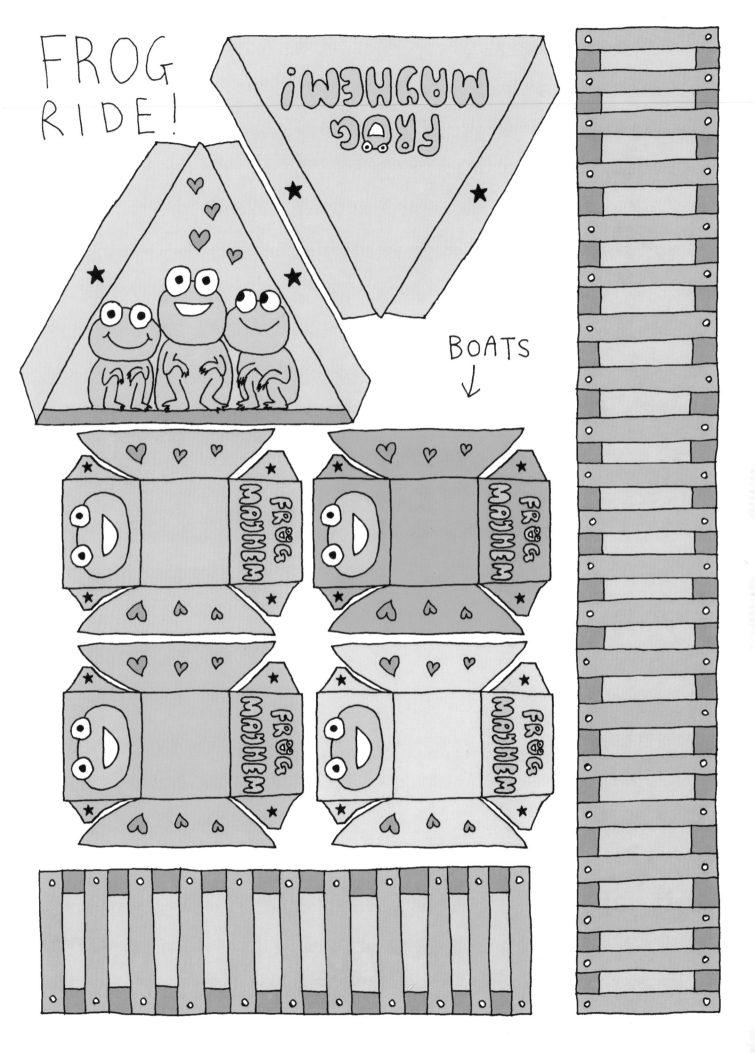

CASTLE FLAGS

FRONT

BACK

MIDDLE PIECE (FRONT)

WIZARD'S CASTLE!

TOWER 1

← TOWER 2

CONNECTING WALL A
↙

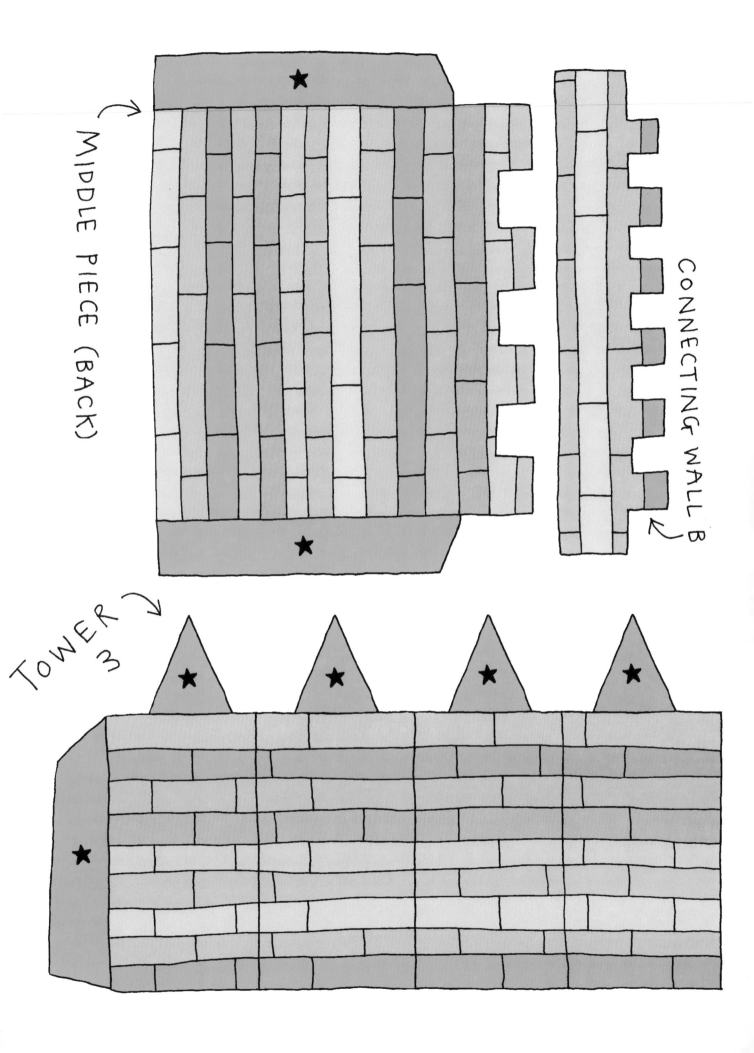

MIDDLE PIECE (BACK)

CONNECTING WALL B

TOWER 3

TOWER 5
TOWER 4

WALKWAY
(FOR MIDDLE
PIECES)

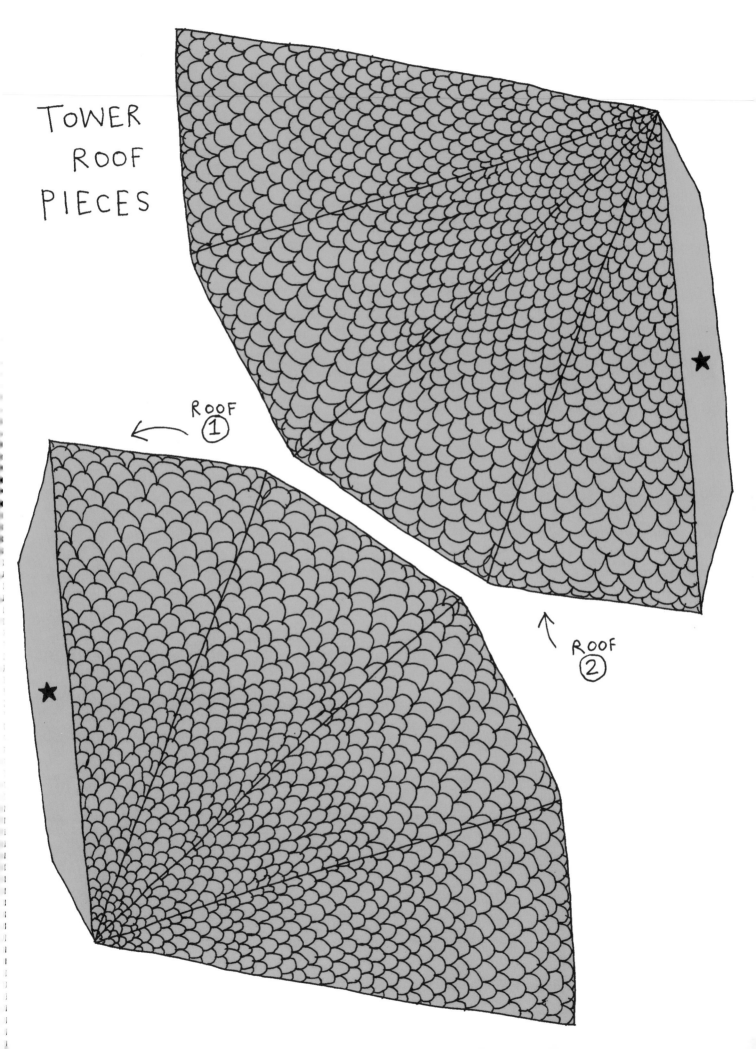

TOWER
ROOF
PIECES

ROOF
①

ROOF
②

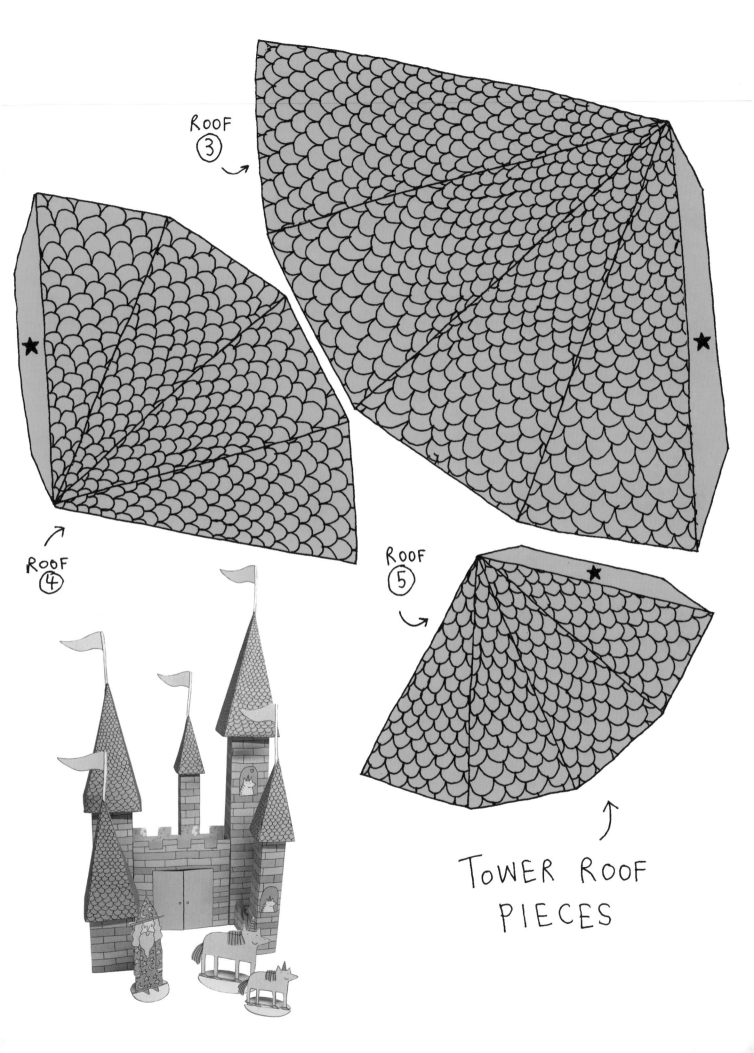

ROOF ③

ROOF ④

ROOF ⑤

TOWER ROOF
PIECES

# BIG UNICORN!

BACK · FRONT

# SMALL UNICORN!

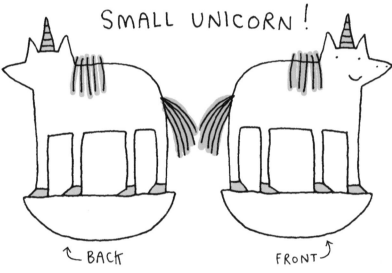

← BACK    FRONT ↗

# KEITH THE WIZARD

FRONT    BACK

NOW WE'VE FINISHED BUILDING LIZZNEYLAND, WHAT SHOULD WE DO?

LET'S INVENT OUR OWN PARKS NOW!

WHAT DO YOU MEAN?

WELL... THIS THEME PARK IS BASED ON LIZZ LUNNEY'S COMICS AND CHARACTERS...

...MOUNTAINS, CATS, KEITH THE WIZARD AND HIS UNICORNS, ETC...

NOW WE CAN INVENT OUR OWN WORLD!

WOW!

HERE'S A PENCIL.

I'M NOT SO GREAT AT DRAWING...

DOESN'T MATTER!

THESE ARE MAGICAL PENCILS THAT WILL HELP US TO DRAW!

YIPPEE!

ALSO THIS BOOK HAS PAGES TO HELP CREATE NEW IDEAS!

COOL!

WOW! WE CAN USE THESE FORMS TO INVENT + PLAN OUR OWN PARKS!

MY PARK IS CALLED "TIGER ZONE!" THE WHOLE PARK IS TIGER-THEMED WITH A BIG CAT PARADE!

COOL! MINE IS CALLED "BORINGWORLD."

"BORINGWORLD?" THAT DOESN'T SOUND VERY FUN...

IT'S NOT! THERE ARE NO RIDES. NOTHING TO DO. THE WHOLE PARK IS ONE LONG LINE...

MAYBE YOU SHOULD TRY AGAIN...

I DON'T HAVE ANY OTHER IDEAS...

WELL, WHAT DO YOU LIKE?

I LOVE ICE CREAM!

SO DESIGN AN ICE CREAM THEME PARK! WOW!!

I CAN HAVE A STRAWBERRY ICE CREAM ROLLER COASTER! A WAFFLE CONE FERRIS WHEEL! OOOH, A RAINBOW ICE STAND!

I WOULD LOVE TO GO TO AN ICE CREAM PARK!

YOU CAN BUILD IT!

NAME OF PARK  LIZZNEYLAND

CHARACTERS  KEITH THE WIZARD
UNICORNS
SANDWICH HEAD
SPACE GUY

THEME  LIZZ LUNNEY COMICS

OTHER ATTRACTIONS

RIDES  MOUNTAIN ROLLERCOASTER
FROG MAYHEM RIDE
MAGICAL CAROUSEL

CASTLE, STANDS (GIFT + FOOD)
LITTLE TRAIN, GAME MACHINES

---

NAME OF PARK

CHARACTERS

THEME

RIDES

OTHER ATTRACTIONS

---

NAME OF PARK

CHARACTERS

THEME

RIDES

OTHER ATTRACTIONS

---

NAME OF PARK

CHARACTERS

THEME

RIDES

OTHER ATTRACTIONS

DESIGN A LOGO
FOR YOUR PARK:

LIZZNEYLAND

DESIGN A LOGO
FOR YOUR PARK:

DESIGN A LOGO
FOR YOUR PARK:

DESIGN A LOGO
FOR YOUR PARK:

# OTHER IDEAS TO ADD TO THE PARK!
## USE POSTER BOARD TO ADD NEW ITEMS TO YOUR PARK

MAKE A PARADE FOR THE PARK! DESIGN YOUR OWN FLOATS OR ADD CARS TO THE TRAIN!

ADD TRACKS TO THE ROLLER COASTER TO MAKE A MEGA ROLLER COASTER!

DRAW YOUR OWN GUESTS AND CHARACTERS FOR THE PARK!

DESIGN YOUR OWN GIFT SHOP!

IMAGINE SOME SPECIAL EVENTS THAT CAN BE CELEBRATED AT THE THEME PARK!

INVENT YOUR OWN VENDING AND GAME MACHINES!

ASK YOUR PARENT TO SHARE YOUR CREATIONS ONLINE #BUILDYOUROWN OR WATCH TUTORIALS AT LIZZNEYLAND.COM!

Andrews McMeel Publishing
a division of Andrews McMeel Universal
1130 Walnut Street, Kansas City, Missouri 64106

www.andrewsmcmeel.com

19 20 21 22 23 TEN 10 9 8 7 6 5 4 3 2 1

ISBN: 978-1-4494-9632-6

Library of Congress Control Number: 2019930228

Editor: Jean Z. Lucas
Art Director: Holly Swayne
Production Manager: Carol Coe
Production Editor: Margaret Daniels

**Made by:**
1010 Printing International Ltd
26/F, 625 King's Road,
North Point, Hong Kong
1st printing – March 25, 2019

**Attention: Schools and Businesses**
Andrews McMeel books are available at quantity discounts with bulk
purchase for educational, business, or sales promotional use. For information,
please e-mail the Andrews McMeel Publishing Special Sales Department:
specialsales@amuniversal.com.